BLEEDING WORDS

A COLLECTION OF POEMS

KENISHA BAILEY

Copyright © 2021 Kenisha Bailey

All rights reserved. No part of this book may be reproduced, stored, or transmitted by any means—whether auditory, graphic, mechanical, or electronic—without written permission of both publisher and author, except in the case of brief excerpts used in critical articles and reviews. Unauthorized reproduction of any part of this work is illegal and is punishable by law.

To contact the publisher please visit our website.
www.trinityhillspublishing.com
92 Cipero Road
Retrench Village
SanFernando
Trinidad and Tobago

This collection of poems is dedicated to all my impassioned friends and family, who continued to believe in me, even when I doubted myself.

CONTENTS

PART1: WOUNDS
I Told You So	8
When The Storm Subsides	11
The Vindictive Man	13
I Hate You Too	15
He Died With Me On His Mind	17
Drowning	19
Too Quick To Love	20

PART2: HEALING
Baring My Voice	23
The Magic Of The Chameleon	25
Catatonic	26
I Let You In	27
Sugarcoat	29
Letting Go	31
Personal Apology	33

PART3: BEAUTIFUL SCARS
Only In Dreamland	35
'Ghetto' Stigma	39
Try, Try And Try Again	42
Leap Of Faith	44
Instinct	45
Angels On Earth	46
Beauty	47
Timelines	48
God's Puzzle	49

PART 1
WOUNDS

Life burns
Life stings
Life lacerates
Life has purpose

I TOLD YOU SO

Like the end result
of an ectopic pregnancy
my words are muted on beat

Oh I try,
but I'm dismissed for being too young
so instead she turns up the volume of the love song

Time passes
ripping away my
Innocent
Adoration
She is no longer perfect
in my eyes

Now that my glasses were stepped upon
she suddenly seems human-like

But I still remember her hugs
filled with love
the way she watched me
with fascination
I admired her strength
She was so strong
(but I was so young)

I didn't see it coming
but when it arrived
I envisioned the outcome
I summoned it into being
No good can or will come from this.

I felt hurt but she felt bliss

stuck between me
and the lustful grip

Until now

Now she cries everyday
Says that God has a cruel way
Now she thinks
about what's best for her family
Now she can see the depth and danger
of the alluring sea

Now she panics
because she sacrificed her peace
Now she no longer understands me

And I feel badly
for not feeling sorry
what kind of beast am I
to see her suffer and not worry?
Have I shut down
and switched off my humanity?
But I told you so
and now I'm done
pillar of salt behind
I'm moving on

The choice is made.

I must save me.

My warning
made a late dawning

But I told you so

Changed is our relationship
Stained with betrayal
Cynically doubting yet hoping…

I remember her perfection.

WHEN THE STORM SUBSIDES

My body is the boat
that has been tossed
at sea

Silver swords stabbing
through the air
are all aimed at me

My eyes are blinded
by the darkness
of the sky

My heart poured out
all hopes
of a happy tomorrow
into the chasm of emptiness
my plight

Nature turns on itself
that's why I have
no trusted friend
or family
by my side
in this raging storm,
and no dove to bring me
that everlasting green
from a promised land

But if the storm subsides,
would survival be worth
the tormentous ride?

My body is the boat

that has been tossed at sea
chopped off are the weaker parts of me

It has lasted so long
that murky water wells
inside of me

But even my tears
are blown away
by chastising winds
that reprimand me
for not being strong,
reminding me that
I'll be blown away
if I can't hold my ground

I try not to tremble
in the cold
but there is no comforting
myself with the memory of warmth
because I can't remember
what it feels like when
the sun shines

But if just for this moment
my heart won't mind
I'd hope that
Maybe
Maybe I will
Maybe I will see
Maybe I will see the sun rise
when the storm subsides

THE VINDICTIVE MAN

Spite inhabits his mind
and plots with his soul
your demise

He tries to break you
enjoying every millisecond
that you suffer

Draining the youth
from your face
from your hopes
and dreams
separating your ideas
of faith and belief

He tries with all his energy
to pump the vitality from your smiles
until that strained curve
is never reflected in your eyes

You build a defense
Eventually
and rebuild your self esteem
Manually

Then he feigns
remorse, accepts reproach and responsibility
just to claw
at your newfound stability.

If you break
then he wins

playing on the guilt
of all your sins.

If you sin
you err against God only
so let your tear ducts
consider him unworthy.

Reclaim your independence
He has proclaimed his death sentence
to the grave that he meant for you.

Through his manipulation
he becomes his own victim
no peace under the land
for the rascal
Vindictive man.

I HATE YOU TOO

I hated being apart from you
My heart ached
We weren't twins, but I felt like I lost part of me- half of me

I was only six years older
but many times, I assumed the role of mother

I cleaned your vomit
sang you lullabies
rocked you to sleep
taught you how to pray
taught you how to read
picked you up from school

I was your greatest defender
When they didn't believe in you
I believed in you

In my eyes you were destined for greatness
and that's all I ever wanted for you- great things

But you broke my heart as carelessly as you broke your toys
you turned your back on me
screamed you hated me

I see the indifference in your eyes when you regard me
Can you tell me what I did to earn this apathy?
How do I keep loving you,
when every time I try to get close
you stab me,
jab at me?
You always have to slice a slab of me

Now I can no longer roll beads for you
can't utter sincere prayers for you

You say it's hate
I definitely feel the indifference

My heart needs to start its own resistance

It hurts to love you
So I might just… hate you too

HE DIED WITH ME ON HIS MIND

Tic Toc
Tic Toc
Tic Toc

The ticking must have killed
the deafening silence
resounding through the room

He was too handsome
to accept his fate
too arrogant
to admit his guilt
too ashamed to face me

It did not matter that I needed him
He had ideas of leaving me
in what he called 'good hands'
good hearts that hurt me
so many years later

So he sat and drank the poisoned wine
thinking about the innocent eyes
and big smile he was leaving behind

It haunts me to this present time
that he died with me on his mind

THE SHAME IS HIS MY DARLING

Young
Naive
You smile like nothing happened
You live with a day to day fear
that someone knows what you did
(what he did to you)
Your heart is pounding
(pounding with shame)
You hide in the house,
(never wanting to be seen again)
You think that you are at fault
so you never tell
(you think your space is reserved in hell)

Then you see him
(he seems fine)
He laughs and talks
(with no guilt in mind)

So you bury it deep
(as time goes by)
The wound remains
there are no cures
(they cannot see that the shame is not yours)

DROWNING

It's a frightening feeling
to be drowning
That panic that I will not make it

The fear that no one can see
no one will save me

Sometimes I make a scene
kicking and gesticulating frantically

Sometimes I save that energy
and put it into swimming alone
and making it back to shore safely

And sometimes I get tired of the struggle
and I let it be
Sometimes I give in to life drowning me

But I never stay in that place for too long
Ask for help
Keep swimming
Stay strong

TOO QUICK TO LOVE

I can't convince you that I'm worth it
Worthy of your love
your trust
and honesty

You say you want me
and yet you leave me feeling empty
I've poured all my love into you
and you haven't given
any real love back

This attraction between us
could be flourishing
because I give a love that is so nourishing
Too nourishing to have thrown back on my face
Maybe you're not ready for a love
that feeds your growth
a love that sustains

I want you to love freely or not at all
Love is not a game of tug of war

We can build a love that is slow
But I have no interest in building a love
that is shallow

I won't beg to be your safe place
For goodness sake
You're so damn unreliable
My heart can't rely on your love
If I fall will you catch me?
I have a feeling you'll just watch me
hit the ground

Then look at me coldly as you say
that you never asked me for my love

PART 2
HEALING

The healing may be ugly
The healing hurts
But then it becomes beautiful
For you overcame
The ugly lacerations of life
(thus far)
And you are not the same
You are stronger at this point
Than you ever were before

BARING MY VOICE

Somewhere along the line
I became too nervous to speak
Somewhere along the line
I stopped believing in me

I questioned my every thought
I stuttered
couldn't speak

Somewhere along the line
anxiety put its claws on me
And it's been a hard fight
to rid myself of this senseless fright

Then I take a look at nature
It really comforts me
I admire the Savannah
when I take a look at the trees
They're all different
in shapes and sizes
Nevertheless, they're all beautiful indeed

It's okay to think differently
It's okay to be unique
If it's doing no harm at all
It's okay to be a freak

I want to be my true self
I want to make me proud
I want to shake this anxiety
So I can stand out bravely in the crowd

So what if you're different
So what if you disagree
There's enough space in this world
for you to be you
and for me to be me

So if you hear me being loud
smile, don't make a fuss
It took a heck of a long time
for me to let this voice out

THE MAGIC OF THE CHAMELEON

The chameleon is prettier than a poui pink
and the brilliant ocean blue
Roucou red and
the vibrant Savannah greens

Like the chameleon
I'm a survivor
I'm anything I need to be

Adaptation
my greatest weapon
Adaptation
my greatest shield

I do not resist the changes of life
I adapt and I succeed

CATATONIC

How do I express what I feel,
when what I feel are words trapped
inside of me ?

The burden knocks
on my heart
unable to make
its way past keen
Teethed bars

Feelings escape
freely and reluctantly
condensating,
then precipitating
down my cheeks

And I make no attempt
to wipe the saline
water away
for when I lack the ability to move or speak
Catatonic
all I can do is weep

I LET YOU IN

I'm not one to open up
I've never been one to share
I'm not one to truly love
I'm not one to truly care

Most persons get common pleasantries
I have long conversations only when I must
Never liked the deep relationships
reluctant to misplace my trust

I need you to understand
what it means
when I drop my walls
and let you glimpse inside my heart

I thought I found it,
a lasting friendship

Did you really mean it?
Every long embrace

Was it your curiosity that daily masked your face?
Masked your face with friendship
Wet your tongue with lies

I was merely that mysterious girl
that you needed to analyze

I hate that I was fooled
my heart feels so mocked

Such casual indifference

you dare to call love

Time to let go
walk away
Therein no problem lies
the thing I never told you
I'm the master of goodbyes

SUGARCOAT

I hope you shed your sugarcoat
that makes you always nice
A girl can't say what's on her mind, if it's not polite
Do they deserve your politeness?
A question we're told not to ask
Once a lady starts to speak, only pleasantries must depart

I hope you sear your sugarcoat
even if it's hand-stitched and handed-down

To hell with being dainty
the awkward smiles and
tolerating disrespect
while we stay silent
piping on the inside
holding back opinions with regret

I hope you feed them bitter molasses
morning, noon and night
As often as they forget
that they should address you right

Pour it from the depths of your heart
true, unabashed and raw
We've outgrown the fairytales
forget gloves and show the claws

You deserve respect
to feel safe and secure
You don't have to smile
or act all demure

So I hope that you would
I hope that we could
shed
strip
sear
and never again wear
that stupid, sexist sugarcoat

LETTING GO

It hurts to let go
when you've put all you have
into building bonds of love

You can feel the muscles of your heart
ripping apart
A pain that you can't explain
coursing through your body
and you can't explain the tears
or the feeling that this is not the ending
that you deserve
Especially when you fought so hard
to preserve this relationship

And now you're here
shipwrecked and alone

It's an empty gut feeling
a void on the inside

It's the profuse hurting
and slow healing

It's crawling out of bed
not wanting to face the world
without your person

It's the realization
that it's no longer your person

It's the closing of a chapter
trusting that the book is not at its end

That there is more love in you
and more love for you in this world

It's moving on
trusting that you can write your own damn happy ending

PERSONAL APOLOGY

I've had to forgive myself
for all the times I've done me wrong
and for all the times I've let me down

For all the hurting that I've caused
it's now time to take a pause
and make amends

For all the times
I've pretended
lied
been too shy
to let the real me shine
please, forgive me

For all the times
I've let good people go
and couldn't control this huge ego
please, forgive me

For all the times
I've ignored perilous signs
removed the caution tapes
rushed in
and fed my heart to the snakes
please, forgive me

And for all the times
I've stayed in places
where I didn't belong,
and embraced fake connections
please forgive me

PART 3
BEAUTIFUL SCARS

These are my battle scars
I wear them proudly
I will forever carry them with me
They mark the lessons learnt
The peace I've made with myself
And with where I've been

For the hurting and healing
Gave me these scars
As souvenirs of war
And the inner battles
I've won

ONLY IN DREAMLAND

Is the broken attracted to the whole
or does the whole seek out the broken
Haven't I been here before
Incompatible with the sorrowful souls
trying to convince myself that I deserve
someone more like me
someone safe

I know I'm supposed to run from the shells
the empty ones
I've had my heart pulverized
placed on broken glass and fed to me

Why then am I drawn to your darkness?
It's shameful really
The light in me yearns for your bitter soul
Your acrid scent is intoxicating

I'm in the world
but you're of the world

I enjoy my modest desires
I proudly embrace my infantile hope
my belief in everything good

I crave your brazen lust
your horrific cynicism
You've put everything childlike behind you

You make me doubt myself
You shake my reality
You're the earthquake in my dreamland
Part of me hates that you disturb my sleep

Part of me loves that you corrupt my dreams

You make me want to step one foot over the line- maybe just the tip of a toe
You're my dark mirror
everything that I repress
everything that I detest
everything that I turn to religion to redress

Since I've met you
I've dreamed about kissing the lips of Iniquity
You can join us
in a ménage à trois with Lust
Stop!

This is what you do to me
invading my thoughts
driving me crazy

The sound of your name makes me blush
flushed with shame
If only you knew the thoughts I've thought about you

You're magnetic
I feel an almost irresistible pull to your field

I built my walls so high
not knowing you've mastered quantum phasing
Your presence is foreboding

I hear the intelligence when you speak
your every word exudes knowledge
but is deficient in wisdom

Your glances burn holes in my flesh

make me feel raw
and vulnerable to my emotions

Your diction
enunciation
eloquence
and confidence
slowly caress my mind
and take me on a joy ride
to the sweetest intellectual foreplay ever experienced

Your devils play so well with my demons
causing my angels to look on enviously
You have no angels with whom they can play

You shrink my fears
and expand my vices

I foolishly trust you
to remove my lens of innocence
but I won't permit it
because I am enjoying this view

The universe rebels
when our frequencies align
we may attract
but in my heart of hearts
I know you're not mine
You can take me
in lasting reverie
and hide me in your labyrinth

Yes, we can be free
in this state of unreality
But I wish you would bypass me

when I'm awake

'GHETTO' STIGMA

It's the place that is painted black
Where every man-jack presumably owns a gun
Has kidnapped at least one child
or commits some sort of crime

Like an ugly blood thirsty beast
it's a place that elicits fear
Where evil is nurtured and reared
or so the whispers tell
that we're all damned for hell

Maybe it's because we're on a hill
slightly closer to the sun
that they think everyone here has boiling blood

These negative generalizations have
the power to materialize
to grow fangs
to scare goodness into silence
to marginalize
and dehumanize

So, allow me to show you another side

Right on this hill
I learnt the meaning of love
I learnt how to share
how to care
and how to respect the God above

Right on this hill
I learnt to write
to read and to count

and many others can relate to my account

Right from this hill
I have glared out
and admired the beauty of T&T

Right on this hill
I see what you don't see
There are persons who lack love
for them the streets
represent freedom from abuse, despair
and misery

There are those
who will turn anywhere
just to belong
in a society that does not make them feel welcomed

There are those
who fall for lies
because no one dares to enter
to show them the truth

The good here is ignored
but the bad is eminent in society
so, since 'Gangster' has so much fame
Gangster's what some aspire to be

Some are resigned
and accept what others think
to the point where they agree
they don't consider themselves
to be one of us
we're everything they don't want to be
Potential is locked behind the cynicism

of young people who have been rejected and
simply fear rejection

The destructive criticism
is like negative energy
overpowering a circuit
Even though Laventille is not perfect
perfection belongs to no area

So, stop pointing that finger
outstretch both hands
and let's lift each other

But this is in no way me condoning the violence
I want us to engage
brainstorm our solutions
and invite divine guidance

TRY, TRY AND TRY AGAIN

"If you try and you fail
try, try and try again."
Granny's words are echoes from the grave
After all these years, her words still extend to embrace me
to save me
from giving up on a dream
But is it my dream?
Or a dream that expectations built for me?

Quitting has a bad name
but I believe that quitting is the right thing to do
when the thing you're doing is not the right thing for you

Playing it safe is a great mistake
when it wrings out all your creativity from you
and boxes you in

But dreams don't come easy
they make you weary
they test your mettle
but you should never settle

If this dream is born from your heart
it will test you but not tear you apart

Cry if you must
Talk to someone you trust if you must
Scream if you must
Be silent and find peace if you must
You must
You must learn
You must heal

Don't be afraid
Don't be afraid to grow
to learn
to fail
 to try again

Failure is fire
failure can inspire
the genius in us all

LEAP OF FAITH

Leap with your heart wide open
expect the best from life

Leap with your heart wide open
knowing that it is courage not
inertia that fulfills your dreams

Leap with your heart wide open
thank the heavens for creating you

Leap with your heart wide open
you have purpose on this earth
there is something special you were created to do

Leap with your heart wide open
trust in your decisions
trust in your stance

Leap with your heart wide open
even if those close to you do not understand

Leap with your heart wide open
save yourself first then save as many as you can

Leap with your heart wide open
Let hope overpower your fear

Leap with your heart wide open
believe in yourself, give it your best

Leap with your heart wide open
each experience is a stepping stone to your success
So just leap with your heart wide open

INSTINCT

There's a friend who walks with you
wherever you may go
Gives you life advice
if you listen you will know

You'll know where there is danger
You'll know who is not your friend
You'll know when to speak up
You'll know what to defend

If you listen to that impulse
the sage voice within
You'll know you're the only one
who can block you from the win

Instinct is your wisdom
Instinct is your gauge
Instinct reads the energy
in every vibrational space

Instinct walks with you
wherever you may go
Pay attention to this friend
so strong bonds can grow

ANGELS ON EARTH

God put his angels on this earth
(They walk among us)
The angels blend into any place
You can think of
(God takes an interest in us)

God is observant and quiet
He is the best co-pilot
And when he sees us drowning
struggling
he sends His angels to help us

God has sent so many angels
to lend me a helping hand along the way
If it weren't for God's angels
I would not be where I am today

To the persons who have helped me
I'm forever grateful to you

My dream is to be an angel
The joy that generosity pays is indeed gainful

BEAUTY

When I tell you that you're beautiful
it's not your skin I mean

It's the radiance of your presence
It's the truth with which you speak
the confidence you exude
the acceptance of your flaws
You strive for self-improvement
the most beautiful part of all

I love your kindness
depth and openness
the compassion in your heart
Your beauty like your fingerprint
is unique and sets you apart

This beauty is everlasting
and really lifts the bar
When I tell you that you're beautiful
down to your very soul you are

TIMELINES

Everyone has their timelines,
by which they want you to live your life
Everyone has their timelines
and I think it just ain't right

When are you getting married?
Have a baby?
How come you're still in school?
Okay, can I flip a table?
It puts me in a whole mood

I'm living life by my personal clock
ticking at a suitable speed for me
I would never try to control your life
so don't seek to dictate me

I certainly know what I want
I'm not in any haste
Please keep it to yourself
if you don't like my pace

GOD'S PUZZLE

Made in His image
Made in the likeness of God
We have creative power
a direct link to the Source

There is no need to worry
There is no need to fear

Faith can turn all daunting mountains
in our lives
into fountains of whatever we desire

The trick is to aspire to surrender
control of our existence
to the omnipotence of Love
to the omnipotence of God
to the flow of the Spirit dwelling within us

And we are the co-artists of our lives
designing by the thoughts we think
the choices we make
and the energies we embrace

We are the constructive and destructive forces of nature
Natural hazards or natural harmony,
which do we choose to be?

The more we help others
the more we achieve
in making this world
a better place for you and for me

It is about the journey
It is about the Love
It is about the oneness
with yourself and God

One light is a start
Many lights give power
We can change the world
We can start at this hour

If we all give the glory
we will all get the grace
This is bigger than religion
and has nothing to do with race

We are all pieces of the puzzle
that reveals God's face

This collection of poems is an authentic representation of poetry as a tool for self-discovery, self-improvement and self-healing. It delves into the wounds, healing and scars that one cannot escape on this journey called life. The poems are personal in nature, and simultaneously draw from the common well of human experience to which we can all relate.

www.ingramcontent.com/pod-product-compliance
Lightning Source LLC
LaVergne TN
LVHW041557070526
838199LV00046B/2018